Pink Mist

Pink Mist

OWEN SHEERS

NAN A. TALESE | DOUBLEDAY

New York   London   Toronto   Sydney   Auckland

All rights reserved. Published in the United States by Nan A. Talese/Doubleday,
a division of Penguin Random House LLC, New York. Originally published in
hardcover in Great Britain by Faber & Faber, Limited, London, in 2013.

www.nanatalese.com

DOUBLEDAY is a registered trademark of Penguin Random House LLC. Nan A.
Talese and the colophon are trademarks of Penguin Random House LLC.

Jacket design by Emily Mahon
Front-of-jacket image: © donatas1205/Shutterstock

Library of Congress Cataloging-in-Publication Data
Names: Sheers, Owen, [date] author.
Title: Pink mist / Owen Sheers.
Description: First United States edition. | New York : Nan A. Talese/Doubleday, 2017.
Identifiers: LCCN 2016040598 (print) | LCCN 2016046723 (ebook)
| ISBN 9780385541749 (hardcover : alk. paper) | ISBN 9780385541756 (ebook)
| Subjects: | BISAC: POETRY / English, Irish, Scottish, Welsh. | DRAMA / English, Irish,
Scottish, Welsh.
Classification: LCC PR6069.H3994 P56 2017 (print) | LCC PR6069.H3994 (ebook) |
DDC 822/.914—dc23
LC record available at https://lccn.loc.gov/2016040598

1   3   5   7   9   10   8   6   4   2

MANUFACTURED IN THE UNITED STATES OF AMERICA

First United States Edition

For Lyndon,
whose story was almost Arthur's,
and for his mother, Sharon,
who brought him home

Characters

Arthur—20/21 years old.
Taff (Geraint)—20/21 years old. Originally Welsh,
    moved to Bristol as a child.
Hads (Hayden)—20/21 years old.
Gwen—20/21 years old. Arthur's girlfriend.
Lisa—20/21 years old. Taff's wife.
Sarah—Early 40s. Hads' mother.

Glossary

Ally   Irregular kit

Bluey   Military airmail letter

Bootneck   Military slang for the Royal Marines, possibly derived from the eighteenth-century practice of Marines cutting a strip of leather from their boots to wear around their necks to prevent sailors cutting their throats while guarding officers on board British sailing ships

Brize   Royal Air Force Station Brize Norton, Oxfordshire, England

Butt   Welsh colloquial word for mate

CamelBak   Personal hydration system

Corp   Corporal

Face furniture   Facial hair

FOB   Forward Operating Base

Griz   To work through pain

Headley Court   Defence Medical Rehabilitation Centre in Surrey, England

Hellfire   An air-to-surface missile developed primarily for anti-armour use

Herrick   Codename for all British operations in Afghanistan since 2002

Hydrapods   Apache helicopter delivery system for Hydra rockets

ICOM   Integrated communications or unsecured walkie-talkie transmissions

I.E.D.   Improvised Explosive Device

ISO container   Intermodal or freight container

Jäger Bomb   A bomb shot drink originally mixed by dropping a shot of Jägermeister into a glass of beer, but in recent years often more popular with a Red Bull or other energy drink

JTAC   Joint Terminal Attack Controller

Lumi   Illumination mortar

Medivac   Medical evacuation

N.V.G.'s   Night-Vision Goggles

OPTAG   Operational Training and Advisory Group

Painen   Bristol colloquialism, to be in pain

Pitchen   Bristol slang for settling snow

R.P.G.   Rocket-Propelled Grenade

Sangar   A semi-permanent fortified position or watchtower, possibly derived from the Persian slang for "stone"

Terry   British army slang for the Taliban

The Thekla   An ex-cargo ship, now used as a nightclub, moored in the Mud Dock area of Bristol's Floating Harbour

The Tunnels   Underground music venue in Bristol

WIMIK   Weapons Mount Installation Kit, a stripped-down "Wolf" Land Rover fitted with weapons and used as reconnaissance and close-fire support vehicles

Pink Mist

1 AFTER BEFORE

"Gwyr a aeth Gatraeth gan wawr,
   Dygymyrrws eu hoed eu hanianawr."

"Men went to Catterick with the dawn,
   Their ardours shortened their lives."

—*Y Gododdin,* c. 7th century

The sound of wind on a high hill

ARTHUR
Three boys went to Catterick.

It was January,
snow pitchen on the Severn,
turning the brown mud white,
fishermen blowing on their fingerless gloves,
the current pulling their fishing lines tight.
That's how it was the morning when
the three of us did what boys always have
And left our homes for war.

Cos that's what we did, for sure,
make no mistake.
Not going someplace but leaving somewhere.
Getting out, moving on, away from here.
The three of us—Hads, Taff and me,
boarding the train that day,
a suitcase each and a couple of cans,
nervous drags when we changed at Darlington,
those fags going down
quicker than a cider in summer.

Three boys, going to Catterick for basic.
New recruits, crows they called us,
the beastings and learnings and drills all ahead of us.
But already there.
Three boys. Yeah, we might have thought ourselves men,
but we weren't, not yet, not then.
Just three friends who'd once linked arms at school

3

when I was nine, Hads was seven and Taff just eight.
Touring the yard, a chain of three, chanting like fools,
Who wants to play war?
Who wants to play war?

Jump cut to ten years later and the answer was us,
we did.
The game became our way you see—
out, on, off. So yeah, we did.
Three boys, like I said, not men, leaving for Catterick.
Friend us on Facebook and you'll soon see
how quick our profile shots scroll back
from battledress to uniform,
from webbing to sports bag,
from ration pack to lunch box,
from out there to back here.

But we're not scrolling back, not yet anyway.
So three boys then, waiting for the bus at Darlington.
Smoke and winter breaths in the air,
eyeing the other lads, as pale and edgy as us.
None of them looked up to much, but then neither did we.
None of us looked like squaddies or riflemen.
But it was all there, inside us, waiting to happen.
We didn't know it but we were already history.
And history's what we've become.
Not the kind that's recorded or sung, perhaps,
but history still. Our own, histories of one.

And look how far we've come. Full circle.
Back where we left from—Bristol.
Bonfire night, and all of us hiding like dogs
from the whizz-bangs, the bright and sparkly fun.

From up here I can see it all.
The rockets going up from Clevedon,

4

dropping their lights like lumies,
then soft popping ones, rising then falling
down in the city on George the Fifth Fields.
A crowd of orange faces round the fire and the guy,
burning.
Burning.

Can't go there. Or there. So better stay here.
Up on Dundry Hill, under the transmitter.
Under the clear night sky,
the last of the planes coming in to land.
Stars coming out. House windows turning on.
Street lights.
Always a light in the dark.
Even for Hads down there in the Shire,
sitting on his mum's sofa, trousers rolled, curtains drawn,
cast in the aquarium light of the screen
as he plays *Operation Afghan*
to drown out the sound
of the kids on the street mucking around
with bangers and whistles, or anything else
that might make him jump, start or shit hisself.

Look at him, scoring the points, dropping them down,
reloading his mag.
Taking the role, tonight, of a Navy SEAL,
doing on that sofa what we all did, once, for real.

Where's Taff?
Not in the West, that's for sure.
Not in the Shire or out Severn Beach where I used to live.
Not with Lisa either, or with Tom his five-year-old kid.
No, they'll be out Clevedon, or down on the fields,
taking part in the family fun.
But not Taff.

He's deep in the centre, taking cover,
mashing hisself on dubstep in the Tunnels,
dancing alone in the crowd,
feeling the bass vibrate in his ribs,
dropping down pills to mix with his meds.

He's painen, I can tell.
But there's no way he'll surface tonight.
Not with those rockets and fireworks
and all them kids oohing and ahhing,
and him, wanting to duck at every one,
go firm, get on the buckle.
No, Taff'll see the night through down there
deep in the Tunnels, filling his ears
with Forsaken, Headhunter and Pinch.
He knows he can't risk them, the rockets or the drink.
That if he lets 'em, they'll both take a mile off him,
never an inch.

So how'd we get here then?
How'd we close this circle so fast?
If you'll listen I'll tell you.
Cos it was me what got us boarding that train,
what got us leaving not going.
Yeah, it was me who said three boys should go to Catterick,
with snow pitchen on the Severn,
fishermen blowing on their gloves.
My idea, my plan, to link our arms again,
to go on a tour.
To answer the chant of our school days with *us,
us, we want to play war.*

So let's talk about before,
about why I chose the rank and file.
It was January, like I said, 2008,

and I'd been thinking about it for a while.
Every time I came down Colston Avenue
I'd stop at the Army Information Centre,
pause at its window, read the ads,
the jobs, what they said you could do—
JTAC, Infantry, Driver,
Cook, Intelligence, Engineer.
Raise your sights the brochure said.
And one night, I did.

We'd been out on the piss and were going for a kebab
when some scutler of Hads' stopped in her tracks,
bent double and flashing her tramp-stamp,
chucked up her guts.
While we waited for her and her mates,
I read that line again—
Raise your sights.
When I did, I saw my own face,
my ghosted head, right where the picture of a soldier's was,
so now his beret, his uniform, his whole rig was on me,
and I was him.

There were other ghosts too, reflected in that glass,
but they were from my present, not my future or my past.
A Friday-night crowd mashed on cider and pills,
blowing their packets on a night of forgetting,
of pulling and shots.
An ambulance, paramedics.
A drifting litter of boxes and cans,
girls more flesh than dress.
And I didn't want any of it.
The same big night in the same small town,
the Friday carrot at the end of the stick.
I wanted something else—him.
The man looking back at me,

the one with the uniform, the gun.
The one going somewhere, getting something done.

The next day I walked.
I was shacked up with Gwen in St. Paul's back then
so I told her I'd be back for lunch, then left,
early morning.

> GWEN
> But you didn't come back did you?
> That was the day I lost you. I see that now.
> I should have held on to you,
> pulled you back into bed.
> If only I could've seen inside your head.

ARTHUR
But you can't, can you, babe? That's a private place,
and right then, I didn't need you, I needed space.
But I did come back. I did.

> GWEN
> No you didn't. Not Arthur anyhow.
> Some other bloke, perhaps. But not my man.
> You was always leaving, always,
> from that day on.

> Where did you go anyway?

ARTHUR
Out to the bridge, at first.

> GWEN
> What, to—?

ARTHUR

—No! I had you. And Mum.
I was going the other way. I was looking for a life,
not to take one.
And anyway, I'd never do it there.

GWEN

Why? Too common for you?

ARTHUR

No. Just . . .
I saw a man once, who—

GWEN

—You never told me.

ARTHUR

I never told no one. Not even Mum.
I was only twelve, thirteen.
It were early on, mist in the gorge.
I was cycling over to Ashton, the golf course,
to look for lost balls in the rough, when—

He was standing at the edge, smoking a fag,
just past the Samaritans sign.
Looking straight out he was, at the dawn,
but I reckon he heard me,
cos he turned then, see. Turned and looked right at me.

GWEN

How old was he?

ARTHUR

Older, to me I mean. But young now I guess.
Our age about. Twenty-two, twenty-three.

He was calm.
Just looked at me, took one long drag,
stubbed it out, then—

He jumped?

No.
Well, yeah, he did. But more like flew.
Ran a few steps then launched hisself over.
Chest out, arms wide.
A perfect ten-out-of-ten high-board dive.

I didn't stop. Didn't want to see.
But when I got the other side—well, I cried.
His eyes. They stayed with me for years.

GWEN
Why you tellin' me this now, Arthur?
Why only now?

ARTHUR
Cos I thought of him again that day,
when I walked on to the bridge.
How he'd flown like that.
I didn't want to follow him,
but I did want something in his dive.
In *how* he'd done it.
That's all I can say.

GWEN
And that's when you made up your mind?
Because of some bloody jumper?

ARTHUR

No, that was later, up at the church.
But it wasn't me who made the call.
It was the water,
I let the water tell me what to do.

GWEN

Water? What you talking about, Arthur?
All I know is when you came back,
your mind was set.
You were joining—The Rifles,
you told me straight out.

ARTHUR

The water in the pendulum.
You've seen it. You went there with Lisa and Tom.
Taff told me. She wrote him a bluey about it.

GWEN

That thing in St. Mary's? On the wall?

ARTHUR

Yeah, that's the one. It, not me, made the call.
Still don't know how I found myself there, but I did.
Staring at it, the church empty.
A long hollow pipe across the beam of a cross
with water pumped in to make it swing left or right
depending on which way the water is lost.
As good a way as any, that's what I thought.
So I waited till it swung, then came back into line,
then said to myself "Left's the army, to the right's not."

I swear, the water took longer that time.
I watched the tips of the steel beam waver,
dip, lift, like it was taking a breath,

before the water filled to a tipping point,
and the pendulum fell.
To the left.

And that was it. Didn't wait.
Just walked straight back out.
You know the rest.

GWEN
Yeah, I do.
But I still don't know *why,* just the what.

ARTHUR
Think of where we were, Gwen. What we'd got.

GWEN
Each other!

ARTHUR
Yeah. But that gave me more reason, didn't it?
Don't you see?
I did it for us, not for me.

Think about it, Gwen.
I'd been working down Portbury docks for, what?
Over a year by then?
Driving those Mazdas off the container ships,
parking them in perfect lines, like headstones in a cemetery.
Slotting each one, then back for the next.
Every day. Every week. Every month.
One of the largest car parks in Europe,
and just me and two brothers
filling it at one end as it emptied at the other.
I've worked it out, Gwen—how far I drove.
Thousands of miles. But where did I go?

Nowhere.
Never stopped moving from clock on to clock off,
but stayed still all that time, stuck in dry dock.
That's no future, Gwen, and not much of a present either.
And we wanted more, didn't we? Kids, a house, the rest.
The Rifles offered us that.

GWEN

Yeah, heard it all before, Arthur,
"Be the Best."

ARTHUR

And we were. You never saw us, we were. The company,
the Batt—

GWEN

—Enough! I don't want to hear no more.

ARTHUR

It felt different, walking out that door.
I felt different.
Like I'd taken that dive.
You know the first thing I saw?
That rusted piece of tramline, stuck in the grass.
The one that was blown there in the Second World War.
I went up and touched it.
I don't know what for, but I did.
And I felt connected,
like I was part of something already.

As I walked back to Gwen's,
everything had changed in the city.
I'd done nothing, but everything.
It's funny like that, isn't it?
How the only thing that changes is your mind,

but then everything else follows.
How all of it was set in that church.
Not just for me, but for Taff and Hads too.
And for Lisa, and Gwen, and Tom and my mum.
One choice.
Hard to believe it can do so much.
But it can.

I told the lads down the Thekla, next night.
I'd already done it, joined up that afternoon.
Taken the oath, signed on the line.
And it felt good too.
The recruiter, he'd treated me like a man.
Like what I could be, not what I am.
So yeah, I wanted them—Hads, Taff—to feel like that too.

The Thekla was packed. A retro night of old Bristol tunes,
the kinda stuff my mum would play—
Tricky, Portishead, Massive.
An old showboat, moored up in the Mud Dock,
dark waters lapping at its hull,
smells of a ferry and a bar all in one.
A floating steel club, ringing that night
with trip-hop, not dub.

We was on our fourth or fifth cider when I told them,
shouting over the chatter and bass.
They leant in, close to my face.

"I joined up," I said. "Today. 1st Battalion, The Rifles."

Taff got it straight off,
nodding, serious over his pint.
He put his hand on the back of my neck.

TAFF
Good for you butt.
Yeah, I can see that, makes sense. It does.
So when you leave?

ARTHUR
A fortnight. Up to Catterick for basic.

TAFF
For how long?

ARTHUR
Six weeks.

TAFF
And then?

ARTHUR
Could be anything. Don't know where, or when.
They went skiing last winter. Or exercise in the Rockies.

TAFF
And Gwen. She alright with this then?

ARTHUR
Yeah, she is. It's good money innit? And gets better too.

TAFF
Yeah?

ARTHUR
You know, promotion. Or if you go away.

HADS

Away?

ARTHUR

"Yeah," I said, turning to Hads. "Iraq. Afghanistan."

HADS

To war you mean?

ARTHUR

Yeah. They've already been.
But that's why now's so good?
It's like my recruiter said today,
it'll be a chance to do the job
they train you for.
Otherwise it's like going to the fair,
but staying off the rides.
So yeah, I want to go to war.

HADS

You're nuts, man. You serious about this?

ARTHUR

Course I am. Like I said, it's done. I joined today.

TAFF

Two weeks you say? Before you go?

ARTHUR

Yeah. If you joined up now, you could too.

The sound of wind on a high hill

ARTHUR

I could tell Taff was in, he wouldn't say no.
He'd been having a shit time for the last few months.
An apprentice on crap pay to a St. Paul's plumber

16

who got at him all day.
Then back to his high-rise with Lisa and Tom.
He loved them, don't get me wrong.
But it was hard on him too.
Man of the house at just eighteen,
but not earning enough to clear the debt,
get them out of the rough.
Taff was hungry for a change, I could taste it off him.
He wanted more,
and now I'd put it in front of him,
that meant The Rifles, war.

But Hads, well, he was younger than us,
only seventeen back then,
still lived at home with his mum and old man.
Taff took a swig on his cider, looked hard at him.

TAFF
Waddya reckon?

ARTHUR
Hads just looked back, bit his lip,
like he couldn't believe this could happen.
Then he turned away,
stared over the heads of the drinkers and dancers.
He was the youngest, but also the tallest.
Good-looking lad. Somali cheekbones from his dad,
Green eyes from his mum. A one-of-a-kind kinda kid,
which is how we were mates.
I'd seen him defend hisself since he was six,
firing-up much older boys.
You had to give it to him, good with his fists, up for the fight,
even then.
But now—he shook his head, still looking away,
before turning back to say—

HADS

Nah, can't do it, sonner. Not for me.
Just started up at Next innit?
Up at Cribbs Mall.
It's a good job. I ain't gonna throw it away.
I mean, good luck, mate, really,
But nah. Me mum would kill me.
And my old man.
Count me out of this one,
you boys is on your own.

ARTHUR

But the seed was sown.
There in the *Thekla*'s hull, with the cider inside us,
and Massive on the system.
I didn't say nothing to Hads right then,
but I knew, I did.
He would come too.
Cos I mean, what's next after Next?
Hauling his arse up to Cribbs every day.
For what? A couple of years on the floor,
then, if he's lucky, assistant manager, maybe,
after time served, more—
a nicer suit, some girl off the perfume store.
Nah. Hads was made for bigger things. He wouldn't settle.
So when the army set up a stand next week,
right there in the Mall
between the doughnuts and the Disney shop,
Hads kept eyeing it, couldn't stop, catching it every time
the sliding doors opened and shut.
He picked up a brochure on his break.
Read it at home in his bed.
Went back the next day and signed.
Twenty-two years, life on the line.

Taff had already done the same.
So when we left that day,
with snow pitchen on the Severn,
and fishermen blowing on their gloves,
catching the train from out by my mum's,
all three of us were on our way
to become riflemen.
Sharpe's regiment. Attached, back then,
to 30 Commando.
Three boys off to Catterick.
A suitcase each, a couple of cans.
Off to war, like boys always have.
Boarding a train, leaving home,
off to Catterick, to reap what I'd sown.

2 HADS' STORY

The sound of boots on the ground, walking slowly

HADS

We called it Afghan roulette.
Every day, more or less.
Going out on the ground
to take our chances
with what was under it.

Low metal content. Infra-red switches. Trip wires.
Filled with nails, ball-bearings, human shit.
Or old Russian stuff. Anti-tank, pressure-plates.
Or just some bloke on a phone pressing "dial."
Any of it enough
to turn you or your mates
into dust.

It was me who was meant to stop all that.
Up front, slow-sweeping my Vallon left and right.
Listening for the tone
that would stop me in my tracks,
send up my hand to freeze the patrol at my back.

After Catterick I wanted to be a medic.
And after we deployed too,
I kept applying for the course.
But they reckoned I was good at this stuff,
so they kept me at it.
Eighteen, and the lives of the patrol depending on me.
I had dreams.
Missing a massive I.E.D., turning round too late

to see them eaten up by the earth—Arthur, Taff,
the whole section, my mates.
Gone in the blink of a boom,
a cloud of grey ash.

ARTHUR

But you didn't, did you, Hads?
Never missed a thing. At least, not till . . .
They were right. You were good. Had some kind of sense.
You could smell when something was up.
When the atmospherics changed—
locals leaving, birds flying from a tree.
I don't know how you did it, but believe me,
an ant could have farted
and I swear you'd have caught it.

Only wish I'd been as sharp
that night in the *Thekla*, back at the start
when I asked you and Taff if you wanted to join me,
when I planted the seed of that thought in your mind.
Remember where we were? Down in the hull,
on the port side of the boat?
Just inches from that Banksy, sprayed the other side.

I saw it back on R and R.
You know the one. The skeleton rower,
a death's head with a hood,
the prow of his canoe breaking the Plimsoll line.
That's what was on the other side of us
when I told you I'd joined. Right there in the docks
where the press-ganged blokes
had once downed their drinks
only to find the king or queen's coin.
If we'd remembered that rower, would we have sensed it?
How our journey was cursed?

Would his empty sockets, his hands on the oars
have made us more wise?
Would we have known the only coins we'd be taking
were the ones on our tongues, the ones on our eyes?

HADS

No.
You're talking bollocks, Arthur. Again.
We wouldn't have done nothing different
and you know it.
Even if we went back,
we'd still play it the same.
Cos it ain't all bad, is it?
I'll never forget the times we had.
I know myself now. I didn't before.
You were right, I had to get out.
And I always would have,
just happened it was you
who showed me the door.
No more.

ARTHUR

Remember when we first got there?
The plane pitching in steep.
I thought Taff was going to shit hisself.
Even you was pale.

HADS

Yeah, right.

ARTHUR

You was. No shame in saying it now.
I was too. We'd all had OPTAG, but we knew
that was just a sniff of what we were in for.
And then, when we came down that ramp—

HADS
Wham. That heat.

ARTHUR
Like an opened oven door.

HADS
Yank voices.

ARTHUR
Dust on your lips. The landing strip, moonlit. A smell of—

HADS
Afghan. That Afghan smell. Like . . .

ARTHUR
Shit. And burning. Burning shit.

HADS
The looks on the lads going home,
the pats of their hands on our backs,
Their FOB-thinned faces.

ARTHUR
The beards, the moustaches.

HADS
Yeah, well ally, all of them.
Heading for their two days in Cyprus.

ARTHUR
To get pissed, naked, into fights.

HADS
Out of the system before they meet the wife.

ARTHUR
The kids.

HADS
It's the size of Reading you know? Bastion.

ARTHUR
Yeah, and about as shit too.

HADS
Nah. Bastion's got flushing loos.

ARTHUR
And a Pizza Hut, that bar, "Heroes,"
showing the games. Air-con gyms.

HADS
More ISO containers than down the dock.

ARTHUR
Bottling plant, vehicle pits.

HADS
Mocked-up Afghan village.

ARTHUR
Rose Cottage.

HADS
Yeah. Rose Cottage.

ARTHUR
And bloody hot. Half the boys lobster
by the end of that week.

HADS
Remember switching Kev's lotion for oil?

ARTHUR
Poor sod, couldn't work out why he was grilling like that.

HADS
Lost his hands, didn't he?
On patrol from Jackson.

ARTHUR
Yeah. Both off at the wrist.
Now you see them, now you don't.
What kind of fucking joke is that?

HADS
One I'm still telling, mate.

ARTHUR
Shit, sorry, Hads.

OPERATION AFGHAN
Man down! Man down!

ARTHUR
Hads presses pause on the game,
pulls his chair closer to the sofa
and, in one smooth move I'll never get used to,
swings himself up and into the seat,
flicks the brake
and wheels to the bathroom.

Let's give the man some dignity, no need to follow him there.
He does it on his own now, but it's still far from pretty.
Twenty-one, and emptying a bag like he's ninety.

I only see it now, after it all,
but Hads was shaped by war.
I mean even before I cornered him and Taff.
His old man for a start,
came here from the trouble in Somalia,
saw his own father shot, there on the spot, so wanted out.
Settled in Bristol, met Hads' mum,
got hitched, moved into a house in Shirehampton,
one of those built after World War Two,
only meant to last a few years, but still there, standing.
So yeah, the Blitz made Hads' home, and his home made him.
Cos if you're a kid from the Shire
you got roads all over the place—
Outside your door, through your garden,
a motorway over your roof. But the ones in front of you?
They're narrow and few.

And now look at him, wheeling back from the lav—
what war started with his granddad
it's carried on with Hads,
cutting him down from six foot two to four foot three.
Rifleman Hayden Gullet, twenty-one, double amputee.

HADS

I still feel them sometimes.
I'll wake and my ankle'll be itching,
Or I'll need to scrunch my toes. It's frustrating,
cos I can't do nothing can I? Just got to griz it out.
But yeah, my brain still thinks they're there.

ARTHUR

I was there when it happened.
Routine patrol, showing the locals and Terry Taliban
we could still own the ground, take control.
Hads was up front, like he always was,

sweeping his Vallon like a metronome,
low and slow, reading the unseen earth.
And all of us behind him, trying to follow his route,
off the path, across a field.
Two kids just metres away, gathering crops,
and us in full kit; ospreys, packs, helmet and gats,
going firm at the slightest of sounds. It was hot, tense.
Just three hours from the gate,
and I'd already drained my CamelBak.

The ICOM chatter was high, so we were taking it steady.
Hads wasn't happy, so he changed the route again.
The Corp didn't question him, he knew he'd saved us before.
For three months now he'd always brought us home.
But we were jumpy. The Sarge told him to hurry.
The whole patrol was out in the open, in the kill zone.

HADS

I could feel it there, somewhere. Close.
There was a bridge up ahead.
I'd already seen two locals
take the long way to reach it,
avoid the patch we were in.
I was looking for a sign—
some crossed sticks, a pile of stones.
That would be there too, somewhere.
I swung the Vallon again.
Left, right. Left, right.
But nothing, just the midday sun
burning my neck, the boys going firm,
dotting the field,
the terp in the FOB, relaying the comm.
Then—

ARTHUR

The tree line opened up.
Muzzle flashes in the bushes,
the whine and whizz of Afghan wasps
as the rounds came in and our boys hit their buckles,
flat to the ground, faces in the dirt,
doing what they could so's not to get hurt.

HADS

I knew we had to get out, find cover.
I'd seen an irrigation ditch, fifty metres ahead,
if I could find a safe route over—
The boss ordered suppressing fire,
and as the boys laid down a volley of lead
I took a step back.

ARTHUR

I saw it go up.
A sudden tree of earth and smoke,
the ground dropping and rising,
like a heartbeat under the soil.
It threw Hads twenty metres at least.
I can still see him now, as clear as then.
Arching in the air, his arms flung wide,
as if he was back at school again,
high-jumping for top spot—a record-beating Fosbury flop
that left his legs behind.

The sounds of a hospital

SARAH

At first, when they pulled back the curtain
I felt relief.
A wave of warm joy.
There'd been a mistake, a crossing of wires.
This wasn't my boy.

31

How could it be? There'd been a wrong call.
Whoever he was, he didn't look like Hayden at all.
Poor sod didn't have his face.
And yes, I did think of his mother too,
the woman who'd have to take my place.
But when I told them, the nurse asked me
to look at his shoulder.
"Is this," she said, "Hayden's tattoo?"
My stomach dropped. I wanted to be sick.
I traced it with my fingertip
then looked up at his face again.
It was swollen, bruised about the eyes,
four days' growth, singed dark along his chin.
"Yes," I said. "It's him."

I gave him hell when he came back with that new tat.
He was just sixteen but adamant. A coiling dragon,
its tail wrapped about his arm.
It was up to him, he said, now he's a man.
I grounded him for a week, but of course he got out.
He was that kind of kid. Still is.
School couldn't hold him,
more energy than his brother and sister together.
Which is why I was so pleased when he got that job at Next.
At last, I thought, he'd quieten down, earn some cash,
find a girl, maybe, up at the Mall.
Stop hanging out with those older lads.

Some hope in that. That wasn't Hads.
But then, nor was this. A living lie—
This boy in the hospital bed,
dried blood below his ear,
the sheet going flat
a couple of feet too soon,
just nothing after his thighs.

What have they done to him?—That was all I could think.
What have they done to my lad, my boy, my Hads?

HADS
Just this high ringing.
Like something left on too long.
That was all I could hear.
I remember the sky too.
Blue, clear.
But that was all.

They brought me round in Bastion,
then put me under, more or less, for a month.
Induced coma.
Four weeks of living dreams,
of contacts, torture, the lot.
Back home in a flash, but not.

When I finally came to
I thought I was still dreaming.
Of course I was. I'd soon wake again, and maybe again,
until, one day, I'd be back in my life,
the one I knew.
But I was already there, and the day that dawned,
it did so in a second.
It was something in the look of the nurse,
in the way that she said it.

This is you now, Hayden, but think,
it could have been so much worse.
You have to try to count the blessing, not the curse.

I cried.
For two days solid. Didn't eat, didn't sleep.
I'd got no fucking legs.

That was it. One step back and Terry had got me.
Nothing where my legs had been
or in my future either.
It was over, at just eighteen.

And then it wasn't. I still don't know why
but on the third day I stopped.
My eyes were raw and my ribs were sore,
but my mind was clear.
I was only eighteen but I was alive.
I was going to live for loads more years
without legs than I ever had done with.
I'd survived, and if I was going to carry on
I'd better make the living I'd got left worthwhile.
That's what I told myself anyway.
As soon as I did, my worrying switched.
Had the others been hit?
If they had I'd never forgive—

ARTHUR
—No. We were good, and it wasn't your fault.
We all got back that day. JTAC called an Apache in,
emptied its load on that tree line, blew it away.
Back in the FOB though, everything changed.
You were the first, you know?
We'd been lucky. It had been getting hot, but till then . . .

For the rest of the tour all I wanted
was to see them drop.
The other lads too. We wanted revenge.
The older blokes tried to talk us down,
they'd been here before,
but we hadn't.
It wasn't just doing a job any more.
It was about killing them,

for you and all the other shit they'd done.
About stopping their hearts, their brains, their lungs.

SARAH
At least I knew. I wish it hadn't happened, of course.
And he'd promised, just the one tour,
so yes, he was halfway there.
But the waiting had been almost as bad.
The not-hearing for weeks then just minutes on the phone.
I'd turn up the volume when the news was on,
dig my nails into my skin, thinking, "Thank God it's not him."
And then it was.
But yeah, now it had happened, what's done was done.
So we had to look forward, didn't we? What else could we do?
As soon as they'd let us we got him into a chair,
took him off the ward and out,
for a fag and fresh air.

HADS
It had rained the night before.
I'd heard it from my bed against the window.
So when we came out those doors, backwards of course,
that was the first thing to hit me.
That rain-on-tarmac smell.
Summers down the Shire as a kid,
going out to play after a downpour in June.
Then Mum swung me round and I saw the grass,
a strip of it between the two car parks—
greener than I thought any grass could be.
For over four months I hadn't seen a blade,
not like this.
In Afghan there were crops, reeds,
but everything was yellow or brown when we were there.
The ground outside the FOB just dust, bare.

I asked her to push me on to it, and she did,
tipping me back to lift the wheels off the kerb,
till I felt the change, the softness of the turf.
As she looked in her handbag to find us a lighter
I forgot for a second why we were there.
So I reached for it, leant forward from my chair,
but as the blades brushed my fingers,
something was wrong. I kept going,
nothing to stop me.
I hit the ground with my stumps, end on.

ARTHUR

By the time that happened to Hads,
we'd already lost two more lads. I.E.D.'s both.
It was Sangin's bumper crop that year,
and it was us who were harvesting them,
from tree lines and ditches, fields and walls.
Terry himself was becoming a ghost, hardly seen,
but still always there, inside our heads.
He wanted us dead and the feeling was mutual.
Cos yeah, we dropped them in numbers,
but the anger, it only got hotter, deeper,
like a hunger we'd never satisfy,
however many we shot,
however many we saw die.

Time to go.
Hads is swinging from the sofa
into his chair again,
and wheeling himself to the ground-floor room
his parents converted for him.
They'll be back soon, along with his brother and sister,
from the firework display on George the Fifth Fields.
Hads asked them to go there without him.
Nothing worse than being the burden,

so yeah, he told them to go enjoy
the bonfire, the burning guy,
the autumn air, the rockets sailing high.
Back here, he's got his own display anyway,
one he knows is coming as he swings into bed.
Look at him, tensing for it, knowing as soon as his head
hits the pillow and he shuts his eyes—

An I.E.D. explosion

Every time.
He lies there a moment, recovering in its wake,
his heart slowing, before rolling on his side
to try and get some kind of rest.
Let's leave him now, as he curls up under the sheets,
or does what he can.
Hads Gullet, twenty-one, half a tall man trying to sleep,
holding what's left of his legs to his chest,
as he tells himself,
on hearing his family come through the door,
that of the half of him gone and the half of him left,
it isn't the cursed he should count, but the blessed.

3 TAFF'S STORY

Dubstep, loud, then fainter.
Rising footsteps, a door opening, then closing

ARTHUR

Here's Taff,
emerging from the Tunnels back into the light,
rising from his barrow
like a walk-of-shame lover.
A long night of taking cover
from the fireworks and the bottle,
of losing himself in the electro-beat,
of dancing, full-throttle,
of drowning for hours in Bristol dubstep.
Of moving not thinking,
for fear in stopping
he'll remember and weep.

Let's follow him now, as he walks up the street,
past the Empire Museum,
his breath like smoke in the November air,
last night's litter blowing round his feet,
his dancing sweat still drying in his hair.

Wouldn't think him a soldier, would you?
But he was. One of the best, right from the off.
Taff loved basic, he did. He was ripe for it.
That night in the *Thekla,*
he'd agreed before he'd finished his pint.
Like he'd said, it made sense.
Time for us to get out of here.

And we did.
But then we came back,
bringing "there" with us—
the anger, the dreams, the dead.

> TAFF
>
> Aw, shut it, Arthur!
> It's first thing in the morning,
> I could do without you inside my head.
> Can't you leave me alone, just for a bit?
> Always bloody talking. Give it a rest.
> And when did you get so wise anyway?
> You was so thick at school
> you couldn't pass a urine test.

ARTHUR
Just saying, that's all. You were good, the best,
and you know it.

> TAFF
>
> Were. You said it. In the past innit? History.

ARTHUR
Yeah? Looks like it too. If that's the case
why you been hiding down there all night?

> TAFF
>
> I wasn't bloody hiding, right?
> Just . . . you know how it is.

ARTHUR
Yeah. I do. How's Lisa, the kid?

> TAFF
>
> Fine. I'll be seeing him this week.
> He's five now y'know?

ARTHUR
Five!
How old was he when we left? One? Two?

TAFF
Look, Arthur, I gotta go.
Gotta get my head down.
I'm in the project at ten, so yeah,
see you later is it?

ARTHUR
Yeah, alright. See you then.

No, you wouldn't think Taff a soldier.
Not now. The muscle turns to fat after a bit.
And then the meds, they soon add to that.
And the drink.
He must have put on two, three stone since he got back,
but even so, it wasn't his body what got to Taff.

Take this street he's walking down now,
deserted, empty, Sunday-morning dead.
Harmless.
But all Taff's feeling is the threat.
The echo of when a village went like this back there,
when the women and kids melted away.
That's what he's trying to keep at bay,
plugging in his headphones,
turning the volume right up.
Stalling for time till later in the day
when the project will bring him into harbour again.
But right now he's alone, and half of him's on tour,
remembering with a memory that's *now*
the fear, the tension, and of course the four
who didn't make it back with him—
Big Ash, Stevo, Lee and Tim.

Arthur's right, I did love basic.
Everything we were meant to hate—the PT,
drill sergeant shouting in your face,
being woken at three to go on guard,
the route march, the beastings—I loved it, I did.
It was what I'd been waiting for.
It made me, all of it.

I remember, when we were just over halfway through,
going into town with Arthur and Hads,
stopping by a butcher's
while we waited for some of the other lads.
Our first time off base since we'd stepped off that bus,
three boys leaving home for Catterick, nervous, young.
I looked in at the meats what the butcher had hung.
Chickens to the left, beef to the right.
I tapped the glass and pointed to some chicken legs.
"See that," I said to Hads.
"That was us four weeks ago. Scrawny little fuckers."
Then I tapped the window above the shoulders of beef,
heavy with meat, packed around the bone.
"And that," I said, "is what we've become. Strong."
He nodded, cos it was true. We could see ourselves reflected,
the three of us in line, bigger at the shoulder and the chest,
thicker in the neck, an ache in our arms and our thighs.
Just over a month since we'd left, and we'd changed.

ARTHUR
Yeah, they built us up alright.
Built up the muscle, layer by layer,
just as they took us away, layer by layer.
Fair exchange perhaps—
three hots and a cot and a packet of pay,
the promise of duty and seeing the world,

not much, I guess,
for handing them your body
and giving what's left of your mind away.
So yeah, they fattened us up
good and proper,
fattened us up for—

TAFF

—Don't say it, Arthur. Don't.
Cos it ain't right. They made us fit.
That's what they did.
Fit in, and fit for fighting.
Fighting fit.
Anyway, easy for you to say. You didn't have a kid.
I did. So that packet of pay?
Yeah, that made me too,
even more than the training, the uniform, the kit.
Lisa had Tom when we were *sixteen*.
I was a father before I was grown.
So when we came home
it was that pay what made me stand tall.
Not just the rest of it. I was earning, providing,
doing what I can.
I was only eighteen, but those six weeks basic,
they were like years for me.
They made me a man.

LISA

They did. When I saw him again
it wasn't just his body what had changed,
it was Geraint—all of him.
Like something up there had made him whole.
So yeah, the army made him.
But then they broke him too, didn't they?
And who had to pick up the pieces then?

Not all the king's horses I can tell you,
or all the king's men.

It was like suddenly I had two kids, not one.
Geraint, as well as Tom.
Falling asleep on his meds, middle of the day.
Not talking, then next minute having it all to say.
Howling, crying, throwing tantrums.
Waking in the middle of the night,
pissing the bed. They both did that.
Only Tom never hit me when I tried to hold him,
like Geraint did.
Or stared into my eyes, soaked with sweat,
looking at something countries away.
Tom didn't have the last year of his life
flashing like a trailer across his mind all day,
or a habit of letting fags burn to his knuckle,
then blister his skin.
He didn't have this look that said "I'll never let you in."
And he didn't have a father either, or at least
not the one who went away.
He had Geraint instead,
drinking, popping pills, his face tense with pain.
A man who used to be his dad, but now just there,
broken by war into a boy again.

I swear, if I could meet that pilot now,
what I'd do to him—
A bit of his own bloody medicine.
And I'd have the right, too, I reckon.
Cos that night he didn't just take the lives
of Big Ash, Stevo, Lee and Tim.
No, he took Geraint's too. And mine. And Tom's.
And that's why I'd do it,
not for my sake or for Geraint's,
but for my son's.

TAFF

They used to call it "friendly fire,"
but not any more.
Too close to the bone.
So no, it's "blue on blue" now.
That's the words they use,
to describe what happened that night.
Blue on blue.
Blue on blue.
Blue on blue.
However much I say them though,
they don't.

LISA

"Friendly fire."
That's the one still makes more sense to me.
Being hurt by those on your side,
by those meant to protect you,
those meant to love you.
Yeah, that I recognise.
The drink, the shouting, the lies.
The hand on my throat while I slept,
the reaching in panic for the bedside light.
The boy you married
lying by your side but somewhere else—
shrinking, out of sight.

TAFF

It was night.
I mean Afghan night.
No lit windows. No cars. No street lights.
Just a few stars between the clouds and nothing else.
We put up lumis as often as we could—
slow-falling mortars burning bright—
but when each one came down again
so did the darkness, and with it the night.

I was on sangar duty. Half an hour left,
my eyes heavy with sleep.
It had been a bad week.
Hads had caught it just a few days before,
then my company were moved to a checkpoint
a mile from the FOB.
Right from the off, things had been hot.
We were there to stir things up, draw them out,
and it didn't take long—pot shots, shoot and scoot,
R.P.G.'s finding their range.
Most days there was some kind of contact.
I won't lie, I loved it again.
Like Arthur had said in the *Thekla* that night,
it was doing our job. What they'd trained us for.
And a chance to pay them back,
for Hads and what they'd done to him.

A few days before it happened
a patrol came under fire.
R.P.G.'s from a compound,
hitting nearer and nearer, too close to the wire.
I was spotter for the mortars, so we went to work.
I sent them in on some smoke I'd seen,
between two trees, over a wall:
One—fell short.
Two—went wide.
Three—direct hit.
Four—to make sure.

But I was wrong. Cos Terry wasn't in there at all.
Just a farmer, his wife and their granddaughter.
Two years old, same age as Tom.

They brought her in with shrapnel to her stomach,
a shark-fin of metal sticking out her navel.

She had burns too, all up her sides.
The medic did what he could, which wasn't enough.
She died.

We'd killed their cow too and smashed up their home,
So the liaison officer filled out the forms, paid out the bills,
and then they left.
I can still see his face, even now.
An outdoor man, skin leathered by the sun.
The way he unwrapped the end of his turban
to wipe at his eyes, raw with what we'd done.
I've wondered since if what happened next
was some kind of punishment.
But I know that isn't how it works.
That there is no one watching,
that the good lads will die, lose their limbs
while the nasty bastards go home whole.
But after I'd seen what I saw, after that,
well, you want to put some order on it all,
find a pattern, a god,
some kind of law.

ARTHUR
But you can't, can you, Taff?
Reports do that. History books do that.
But you and me, we know,
it's another word for chaos, war.
It's like they teach us:
no plan survives a contact.

TAFF
Anyway, like I said, I was on the sangar, keeping watch,
eyes heavy, when at the end of one of those lumi drops,
they attacked. Full contact, on three sides.
Small arms, R.P.G.'s, a 50 cal.

Accurate too, biting at my sandbags,
kicking up dirt from the wall.
Quick as we could we set up a defensive shoot—
flares, rockets, tracer fire.

There's a smell to battle. You learn it.
The certain tang of an R.P.G.
The dust and grit of an I.E.D.
The bitter scent of your own hot gat.
The oily hint of a machine-gun belt.
But that night, suddenly,
there was something else.

LISA

"Let them have it."
That's what the Apache pilot said.
American, called in for support.
Thought he'd found a nest of Taliban.
And he almost did,
if he hadn't been off course.
He had authorisation.
Yeah, the inquiry told us that too.
And once he did, he opened up. Blue on blue.
Chain-gun, four Hellfires and two Hydrapods.
Turning his dark screen white
as his nose-mounted sensor
traced the bodies running into the night.
Big Ash, Stevo, Lee, Tim.
And you, my love. And you.
Friendly, friendly fire.
Blue on blue.

TAFF

I was blown off the wall. Broke my back in the fall.
When I came round the first thing I saw

was a pair of plastic chairs up against a tree,
lit up by the fires, the burning tents, the flares.
Like the ones we got in the garden they were,
one blue, one green.
Just the night before, Stevo and Lee had sat in them
playing their guitars, all night long.
But all I could hear, lying there, wasn't them,
it was a dubstep song—
"Get Up" by Pinch, loud in my ears,
like I had my headphones on,
banging away as that chopper smashed up our camp.
I stared at those two empty chairs, and as I did
the blue one started turning purple, and the green one brown.
They went hazy too, like they were going out of focus.
It was all still going down—that Apache firing off all he'd got,
but all I could hear was Pinch in my head,
and all I could watch was those two plastic chairs,
empty, lit up by the fires,
turning reddish brown and purple red.

I didn't know it at the time, but it was pink mist doing it.
Drifting across from where the first Hellfire hit.
Pink mist. Clouding my view.
That's the last I remember from that blue on blue.
Those two garden chairs, turning, then nothing.
Just a tightening of light and a heaviness of air.

LISA
Pink mist. That's what they call it.
When one of your mates hasn't just bought it,
but goes in a flash, from being there to not.
A direct hit. An I.E.D. An R.P.G. stuck in the gut.
However it happens you open your eyes
and that's all they are.
A fine spray of pink, a delicate mist

51

as if some genie has granted a wish.
There, and then not.
A dirty trick you pray isn't true.
White heat. Code red. Pink mist.
Blue on blue on blue.

4 ARTHUR'S STORY

ARTHUR

They called me King.
Arthur. Get it? Everyone gets a nickname.
And that was mine. King.
Rifleman Arthur Brown 256543.
But to the lads in the battalion, always King or Kingy.

New name for a new family. That's how it works,
and at first, don't get me wrong, that's what I loved.
A tightening down of the pride and the bond.
It starts with your regiment—their history, their badge.
Then as you go on, it's a deepening
of where you belong.
Your battalion, your company, your platoon, your section,
all the way down to your four-man fire team.
Until that's what you're fighting for.
The man on your left and the man on your right.
Forget queen or country, the mission or belief.
It's more about keeping your mates alive.
Or avenging the ones who've already died.
Cos that's what fuels war, though no one will say it.
Love, and grief, its rougher underside.

It's ironic really. The whole thing was my plan,
for us to link our arms again, join up together.
And at first it worked for Hads and Taff.
I mean, Hads found his skill as a Vallon man,
and a pride in each patrol that he brought home.
And Taff—he was just up for the fight from the off,
and he was good at it too,

even better after what happened to Hads.
But me? Yeah I enjoyed it, no denying that.
The contacts were a buzz—the real thing, no safety locks,
and sure beat parking Mazdas down Portbury Docks.
But fighting's ninety per cent waiting,
and when you've got that much time, you think.
And that's when the trouble starts.
Cos we're privates, aren't we?
And that's not our job.

There's this language card we got, before we deployed.
Part of the Aide Memoire for Herrick nine.
Mine's in a box now, up at my mum's,
but if she ever dug it out she'd see
how those pages of Pashtun and Dari,
illustrated with pictures,
tell the story of our time out there,
like a kid's cartoon book of modern warfare.

Hello—*Salaam*

How are you?—*Chetoor astayn?*

I—*Ma*

You—*Shumaa*

They—*Oonaa*

Do you need help?—*Koumak kaar daarayn?*

Stop or I'll shoot—*Drezh yaa za daz kawam*

Do you need water?—*Ao kaar daarayn?*

You are under arrest—*Bandeet maykonum*

Man—*Saray*

Woman—*Zan*

Child—*Halak*

Human bomb—*Insaani bam*

56

Where is the pain?—*Dard cheri day?*
Blood—*Khoon*
Dead—*Maray*
Go home—*Khaana burayn*
Shot—*Wishtalay*
Go home—*Korta dzai*
One at a time—*Pa waar yao*
One at a time.

Five months into our six-month tour
and I was on my own.
Hads and Taff, both gone. Medivaced to Bastion,
then, in a matter of hours, home.

I was sure I was next, but I was wrong.
Somehow my "if" never became "when."
At least, not then. We lost others.
A sniper's bullet, a roadside bomb.
Our tour was becoming the worst so far.
And then I left it, just like that,
two weeks, R and R.

We landed through cloud into Brize,
Afghan dust on our boots, our packs.
I flew in with a bunch of marines, back for good,
or until they scratched that combat itch
and volunteered again, like many would.
They were quiet, tanned by the Afghan sun.
A cautious look in their eyes as we waited
with our trolleys around the baggage belt.
Just like a regular airport, until you see the sign—
"Weapon Collection Point,"
and then, in customs, a couple of wounded guys
here to meet their mates, dressed in civvies,

handing out plastic beakers of port,
one prosthetic leg each
showing from under their football shorts.

And then through the arrival doors—
girls in high heels and dresses,
made-up for a Friday night
waiting red-eyed in the morning grey
to see and hold their man again.
Babies who'd never smelt their dad.
Kids, holding painted sheets or flags.
Parents biting their nails, waiting, waiting,
for those doors to slide open,
and for the next to be him,
their lad, safe at last, and back.

I hope they were, but I know I wasn't. No.
I was still there, course I was.
Worrying about the boys,
seeing all sorts of shit when I closed my eyes.
That's why Gwen didn't come.
I told her, I needed time.
And as I shouldered my kit, walked past the Spar,
with its "Real Deal" signs and two-for-ones,
I knew I was right.
Time to drag myself from there to here,
to come home proper from the war.

GWEN

You didn't even come to mine,
when you got into town.

ARTHUR

I told you. I had to see Mum.
She was in a bad way.

GWEN

And me? Hadn't heard from you for weeks.
And after seeing Hads with no legs
and then the mess they made of Taff.
Arthur, I'd been worried sick for months.

ARTHUR

I know, babe, I know.
And I'm sorry.
But what's done—

GWEN

—Is done. Yeah. I know.
And now you're gone.

ARTHUR

Don't say that, Gwen.
I'm here, ain't I? Talking to you?

GWEN

It's not the same, Arthur.
I hear you, it's true.
I don't know . . . You were gone
from the day you joined.
I mean, remember what that was like?
You, coming back on R and R?

ARTHUR

Yeah. I do.

I checked into a hotel outside Brize,
lay on the bed till dawn, scared to close my eyes.
Then got the bus to Severn Beach, first thing.
When I got there the place was empty, nothing.
Severn Beach. End of the line, literally.

Just the bridge disappearing towards Wales,
and the river, wide as a sea, sluggish under it.
Not even the fishermen yet, hooking their bait,
casting their lines. Just the houses, all safe and sealed.
Severn Beach—it's where I'm from, since the age of one.
But . . . I may as well have been back in the field,
on patrol, or in some village in Afghan.
It all looked so strange, unreal.

I let myself in, dropped my kit to the floor,
then climbed the stairs, quiet, so's not to wake Mum.
I opened the door to my bedroom.
Footie posters on the wall. The same checked duvet.
A kid's room, a flashback to before this began.

Then, before I know it I'm on my knees,
opening the bottom drawer in the chest,
pulling out old T-shirts and vests
to uncover, under them, a row of eggs,
blown and bedded in their cotton-wool nests.

We had this thing, me, Taff and Hads,
out by the bridge in Clifton,
the one where I'd seen that bloke take flight.
We'd dare each other to touch bits of rock,
pushing each other further and further
out on to the open limestone cliffs.
"That bit there, with the moss."
"That white patch, the outcrop." That kinda thing.

One day I thought I'd give them a scare,
so I climbed further out, past the dare.
Went right out of sight,
slipping in under an overhang,

then sitting tight as they shouted my name,
shitting themselves I'd dropped and they'd never see me again.
Stupid, really. Still don't know why, but I'm glad I did.
Cos it was only then that I noticed the bird.
A peregrine. Circling above me in the gorge,
screeching a repeating cry.
I looked to my right, and I saw why.
Her nest, scraped out of soil on the ledge.
And inside, right in the middle,
two perfect brown, speckled eggs.

Hads and Taff were still shouting for me
but I couldn't hear them no more.
I edged along closer and, again I don't know why,
reached out and took one, still warm.

And now, three years later, here it was again,
in my T-shirt drawer.
The first of twelve eggs I collected that spring.
Heron, jackdaw, crow, lapwing.
But the best was always hers, that peregrine's.
I knew it was wrong, even then,
but I was sixteen and wanted something just mine,
a secret I shared with no one.
And maybe that's why on that R and R
I went straight back to them,
cos each one, though empty, was full
with the feel of the day when I found it.
The touch of the wind, the taste of the rain.
Each was a moment alone, again.
A stealing of an egg, and more.

I put my hand into the drawer.
Picked up the heron's, a pale sky blue.
Barely there on my palm, smooth and cool.

I closed my eyes and tried to see that day again.
March, I was bunking off from school.
A breeze in the reeds, the water over my boots—

A stupid thing to do.
To think I could get away so easily.
No chance. As soon as my eyes were shut,
I saw them instead. Those two Yanks,
the ones who said they'd take our place,
who drove on ahead to the front of the convoy,
then round a corner where . . .
By the time we got there
their Humvee was a ball of flame
burning in the middle of the street.
I saw them climb out. Both on fire.
They ran, who knows why, but they did.
Two burning guys, puppets of flame.
The first, blinded, ran into a wall,
tried to stub himself out, then fell.
The other carried on down the street,
ten, twenty feet, before dropping to his knees.
He held his arms out for a moment,
a flaming cross,
then tipped forward, on to his face,
and died.

I opened my eyes.
Sweat on my wrists.
I was back in my childhood room,
footie posters on the wall,
my opened palm closed into a fist.
The pale blue shards of the heron's egg
scattered inside the drawer,
like a broken promise.

GWEN

That night, when you finally came home,
I felt like that egg in your palm,
crushed to the bone.

We'd waited so long.
We'd joked about it,
I'd even sent you porn,

but we both knew
this could be us at our best.
Together, tender, close.

My hands on your back,
my breaths on your chest.
I used to feel blessed

when we did it.
And I know you did too.
Stunned by how easily

we made one out of two.

But not any more.
Afterwards, I wanted to weep.
But I didn't want to show you that.

I'd expected lust, yes.
But it wasn't. It was anger,
and not spent either,

but still there, as you pulled out of me
and sat on the edge of the bed,
getting dressed.

"We going out?"
That's all you said.
Like nothing had happened.

"Yeah," I replied.
Trying to understand
what it was that had died.

Looking back though,
perhaps you were right.
Cos nothing is what it was.

Nothing—
that's what you filled me with
that night.

ARTHUR

We went out. Gwen had set it all up.
The V-Shed down in the harbour,
a Saturday night.

It was the last thing I wanted,
but I wanted her too. I did,
so I went along with what she said.

It was all the old crew,
different haircuts and clothes, that's all.
Drinking, dancing, and who can blame them?

They weren't doing anything wrong,
just singing along to Saturday's song,
drinking to forget, drinking to belong.

Downstairs was rammed, so we went up instead.
I tried my best to hold it together,
but it was like I wasn't there,

like I was alone, in my own weather,
not whatever the others were in.
I downed my pint, looked over the scene,

but instead of groups of lads down there
I saw platoons, sections, fire teams.
Young bodies waiting to be taken apart.

I turned to the bar. Started reading the drinks,
the menus, learning them by heart,
which was working till I got to the Jäger Bomb list.

Skittle bomb
Glitter bomb
Berry bomb
Cherry bomb
Fireball.

And that was all it took
to see them again,
those two Yanks, burning in the street.

I ran straight to the gents,
stuck my head in the bowl
and chucked up my guts.

And that's when I knew.
I had to sort this, and soon.
And the very next morning, I did.

GWEN

He went to the woods.
Took his kit, a sheet of tarpaulin,
and left, early.
I don't even think he slept in the bed.

65

ARTHUR

You knew that?

GWEN

Yeah, of course.

ARTHUR

You never said . . .

GWEN

Well, I was starting to get it.
I knew I couldn't keep . . . The way
you spoke that night, in your sleep.

ARTHUR

I did?

GWEN

Yeah, stuff about crosses and Humvees.
And Hads. You called for him twice.
So yeah, I think I understood,
why you had to go and sleep in the woods.
I just hoped it would work,
so when you came back—

ARTHUR

I was better, wasn't I?
Than before?

GWEN

Yeah. You were.
I saw a glimpse of you again
and, well, I had hope, Arthur. Then.

ARTHUR
And you were right to, Gwen,
You were.

GWEN
But it was only R and R, wasn't it?
You weren't back yet, not for good.
So it was just a taste. You in my bed,
then in the woods, then—gone. Again.

The engine of a bus, starting

GWEN
I didn't know you could be so healthy
and still feel such pain.
He was just beginning to be himself,
and now he was off.

ARTHUR
Just one month more.

GWEN
That's what he said,
whispered into my ear
as I hugged him goodbye.

ARTHUR
Four weeks. Then it's done.

GWEN
I held on to him, nodded into his chest,
afraid of what I'd do if I tried to speak.
They held all I hoped for, those four weeks.
Arthur back, and then the rest of our lives.
I'd ask him to leave The Rifles early,

get out, so we could get on.
And I think he would have too.
We'd get married, have children.
There was just that month to get through.
Then, then I'd make him promise.
Never again. Never again.

ARTHUR

It wouldn't have taken much.
I'd seen and done enough.
I'd answered our childhood call,
the one Hads, Taff and me
used to shout out in school.
Who wants to play war?
Who wants to play war?
We'd said "us,"
I'd made sure of that.
And now we had.
But this—saying goodbye to Gwen, again.
This wasn't in the brochure.
Or the worry on the face of my mum,
or the thickening of tears in my chest
as I looked out the window
and saw them both waving,
and Gwen still crying,
as if that, a disappearing bus,
was the last they'd ever see of me.

Which it was.

5 HOME TO ROOST

Military vehicles rolling out of a compound.
Radio chatter. The howling of dogs

ARTHUR

Sometimes at night, around Sangin, Kajaki,
they'd howl like dogs. To communicate.
We had our radios, our channels.
They had the calls of animals,
the darkness, a terrain they knew,
black and green through our N.V.G.'s,
like the world had turned computer screen.

I'd been back a week, so had just three to go
when one night we were sent on an op,
supporting J Company, 30 Commando.
I knew this one was going to be hot.
Those bootnecks, they tend to be at the front of stuff.
A strange lot, mind, the Corps—
a dress and a thong in every kitbag,
think nothing of wandering round camp
dressed like a trannie crossed with a whore.
All of them, thick with face furniture.
But in a fight, you wouldn't want anyone else.
The Yanks are brave enough, sure,
and they have the firepower.
But the length of their tours?
A year, no R and R?
They get spun out.
But this one, with the marines,
yeah, I wanted that.

I volunteered for top cover,
manning the WIMIK's 50 cal.
If it all kicked off, I wanted to be the one
who'd give Terry hell.

GWEN

You had three weeks left.
Why? Why would you do that?

ARTHUR

Before I went back, I went to see Taff and Hads.
They were both doing rehab in Headley Court.
I had to see them. I mean, how they were—
It was my fault.

TAFF

No it wasn't, Arthur.

HADS

You know that isn't true.

ARTHUR

It was. End of.
It was me who put it in front of you.

When I got down there Hads was in physio
having massage on his scars,
so I went to the gym, to wait for him.
Apart from one bloke, it was empty.
He was trying to walk between two parallel bars—
regimental T-shirt, shorts, his amputated thighs
in two plastic sockets,
then an inch of steel on a rubber square.
That's all.
"Stumpies" they call them,

what you first wear
when learning how to walk again.
His back and head were drenched with sweat
as he shifted his weight on to one,
then the other,
moving each time just an inch or two.
I could tell he'd been a big fella,
Six-three, six-four?
Now, only as high as my belt, no more.

HADS
Still got yours then?

ARTHUR
I turned and saw Hads,
wheeling towards me in his chair,
the wounds on his arms still healing
and his board shorts rolled,
to show where his legs weren't there.
"Hads! You bastard!" I said to him.
"Christ, you gave us a scare."
Then I knelt and held him,
didn't want to let go.
"You seen Taff yet?" he said
speaking into my shoulder.
I pulled away—"No."
Hads shook his head. "You should,"
he said. "Before you go."

LISA
The first time I saw him I wanted to be sick.
Covered in tubes, his arms all burnt,
his stomach a cross-hatch of scars and stitches.
He was in a coma. He'd woken once, attacked his nurse,
screaming he'd been captured.

She told me he wasn't the first.
"I'm Pakistani," she said. "Last thing they know,
they're in the field, so . . ."

But all that. The wounds where he'd been shot.
The burns, the hallucinations, even his back.
All that healed, in the end.
But something else had been hurt,
something the surgeons couldn't reach.
His mind, his soul,
call it what you will,
but that bit of Geraint had gone.

It's been the hardest thing.
I mean, you see him now, walking down the street,
and you'd think him fine.
You can't see the raised pink scars,
the twenty-three ops,
the X-rays more metal than bone.
You'd think he's OK, he's home.
But he's not.
At least, not yet.

ARTHUR

I saw straight away what Hads had meant.
It wasn't the cages round Taff's legs, his back,
the burn on his face, infected—
none of that.
It was the look in his eye,
as if a wire had been disconnected.
That was what got me the most.

So that's why, Gwen. That's why top cover,
cos that's what I took back to Afghan.
Hads with no legs, putting a brave face on,

74

and Taff, screwed over by a blue on blue.
I wanted to hurt someone,
to satisfy that hunger
before I missed my chance,
and came back home to you.

GWEN
I swear I woke just seconds before,
as if I'd been waiting.
My eyes snapped open,
looked at the clock. Four a.m., then—

A doorbell
And I knew. I knew.

ARTHUR
I don't remember any of what happened.
Just those howls, like dogs, as we drove out.
The fields and trees all black and green.
Perhaps some of the very first rounds,
but nothing else.

I had to pick it up all second hand,
as my hearing came back in the chopper,
and then again in Bastion.
How when my driver had reversed
he'd hit a roadside I.E.D.
How the explosion hit a fuel tank, or ammo box
right under me.
Shot me out, like a jack in the box,
Sixty feet. And then how it all kicked off.
Rockets, grenades. The lot.

They took me straight to Rose Cottage.
A special room in the medical centre

deep among the tents and containers of Bastion.
A room for the lads or lasses who'd taken a hit
which even the surgeons on camp couldn't fix.

It was manned, back then, by two blokes,
Staff Sergeants Andy and Tom.
It was them who took me in, off the ambulance,
and into their room.
It smelt of sweet tea.
"That scent," Andy said to me. "It's the eau de toilette. Rose.
The Afghans insist we spray it on their guys."
"Don't worry though, Arthur," Tom added on my other side.
"You'll soon get used to it. We did."
And then they laughed. Not for themselves,
but for me, I could tell. And they carried on talking too,
chatting me through all they'd do,
as they put what they'd found of me on to a shelf,
saying "Sorry it's so cold, Arthur,"
which it was, like a fridge.
Then they said "Sleep well" and slid it shut.
My first night of three in Rose Cottage.

I saw them again just before I left.
When they slid me out into the light,
still passing the time of day
as they placed me in the coffin
that would carry me home.
Always calling me by name.
"Not long now, Arthur."
"You'll be back in no time."
Gently, they lowered the lid,
then, like two maids making a bed,
they unfolded, smoothed and checked for snags,
before draping me in the colours of the flag.

LISA

It was hearing about Arthur
that did it for Geraint,
it was that what tipped him over the edge.
He'd been hitting the bottle, upping his meds.
Sometimes the pain was so bad
he didn't sleep for a week.
Then, when he did,
he'd scream out in bed, shouting for Stevo and Lee,
crying into his hands about fires and pink mist.
He put on weight—the meds again—
which put more strain on his spine.
So what happened that night, in the pub,
it was only a matter of time.
Like ever since he'd got home
there'd been a mine planted in him,
and that poor bloke who'd spilt his pint,
without knowing it, he stepped on it that night.

TAFF

I got a year. The judge said I was lucky,
took my service into account. GBH.
Eighteen stitches to his head.
It was the night I'd heard about Arthur.
I just saw red.

The worst thing?
I missed his funeral, and then his memorial too.
Inside on remand, no bail.
I'd failed, on every front. Out there,
back home, and now saying goodbye to Arthur.
I've never felt so alone.
And Lisa and Tom, what's so screwed up
is that all along, through all those months on tour,
then laid up in a hospital bed,

77

through the dreams and the pain,
it was them who'd kept me going,
the thought of seeing them again.
Tom, almost three, talking now, walking,
he hardly recognised me.
And Lisa—well, she's still serving her tour.
Been on it for years now, with no R and R,
ever since I joined and walked out the door.

So I can't blame her really,
for not letting me walk back through it again.
She wanted proof I'd changed and,
the truth is, I hadn't.
Prison's not the place for change.
It's for getting through, surviving.
A thickening of the skin.
When I was released, God knows, she tried,
but I wouldn't let her in.

I was on the streets for six months. Homeless.
Fitting, in a way. I mean, I hadn't come home,
not in my head,
so why should anyone give me a bed?
And I wasn't alone.
There's a spread of regiments under those blankets—
Horse Guards, Paras, Royal Engineers.
And a spread of wars too—
Falklands, Gulf, Northern Ireland, Iraq.
Yeah, you walk this country's streets
and there's our history, under your feet.
I'd still be there too, if it wasn't for Ken.
Ex-marine, touring the pavements and alleys at night,
looking for people like us.
Soldiers who'd fallen, not in the field, but out of sight.
First time he spoke to me, I thought it was bollocks.

Who the hell was this? Broken nose, calling me mate.
Said he wanted to help me, get me up on my feet.
I told him to stick it. I'd heard it before.
Just pulled the bag over my head
and went back to sleep on the concrete floor.

But he didn't give up.
Next time was a hostel. Terrible place.
I thought the noise would kill me before anything else.
Ken found me again, sat on the edge of my bed,
and said as such.
"Mate, you stay here, on the streets, you'll die.
I've seen it happen. It's no way to go. Not for a soldier,
or for any man. Come on, pack your bags.
I've got a van outside. Let's go."

So I did. He fixed me up with somewhere better,
then showed me his project down in Bedminster.
Twelve vets, building a home,
from foundation to roof.
He took me to the foreman's office,
gave me a tea, asked if I wanted in.
I felt something give, a thinning of that thickened skin.
I said I did.
He nodded, shook my hand. "Good," he said.
"Let's build somewhere to live."

SARAH

It was different for Hads.
I mean, I know what happened to Taff,
but when we heard about Arthur, Hads went the other way.
He'd only been home for a couple of weeks.
We was all getting used to the change—the chair,
me helping him in the lav, like when he was small.
He was quiet, and didn't go nowhere.

Just sat at the window, watching,
as if he was scared of what he'd find out there.
Me and his dad didn't know what to do.
We didn't want to push him out too soon, but—
Then the news about Arthur came.
Hads' first thoughts were for Gwen and his mum.
He called them both, right off, then,
when he'd finished on the phone, broke down.
The next day, though, he'd changed.
"I want to go out, Mum," he said. "Get a suit an' tie,
for Arthur's coming home."
And that's when I knew he'd be OK.
It became like a goal.
Gwen, see, she'd asked him to be at the funeral.
But just being there, that wasn't enough for Hads.

HADS

I wanted to stand. Beside his grave.
I might have lost both legs,
and the doctors said it was still far too soon,
but I didn't care. Just for a couple of seconds,
I wanted to be there, full height, for him, for Gwen.
And I did.
They said my spine wouldn't take it,
my wounds weren't healed.
And they weren't.
I bled into the sockets of those two prosthetics.
But I stood, with crutches, beside Gwen and Arthur's mum.
When the flag was folded and handed to them,
as his coffin was lowered and they played last post.
I stood, to say goodbye to my friend.

In a way he'd saved me again,
just like when we'd first met. When I was six—
a bunch of older lads calling me nigger, firing me up.

I was holding my own, but then Arthur stepped in,
took me home.
And now he'd got me home again.
Cos after that day, I got my shit together.
I still don't walk, not yet, but I will.
And in my chair, you should see me now—
My high-jump days were done, so I went for basketball.
It used to be a joke, in Headley Court,
how the MoD was good for wheelchair sport.
Well, now I've made that joke come true.
For me, my mum, old man. And for you, Arthur.
For you.

GWEN

It's been over two years.
People say I should move on. But how can I?
I still hear him, so for me he isn't gone.
He's here, in my head, my memories
and, just about, in the smell on the clothes
he left on the chair.
In videos on my phone,
in the messages I still can't delete.
So no, not gone.

TAFF

For me it's like we're back on the cliffs
and we've dared him to touch
some rock far out.

HADS

But he's gone that bit further again,
dropped out of sight, so we can't see him.

TAFF

But we know he's still there, on the cliff,
holding on.

HADS

Out of sight, but there. Not gone.

ARTHUR

I watch them, talk to them,
and sometimes they talk back too.
Gwen whispers into her pillow.
Taff shows me his lad, little Tom,
and Hads, when he can't sleep
he tells me stuff.
How he worries he'll never get a girl.
Cos that blast, it took more than just his legs.
But he's good, he's soldiering on,
partly for him, but more for his mum.
And Lisa's talking to Taff again,
I saw them laugh the other day,
so who knows, once he's built his home,
perhaps he'll have another place to stay.

And me? Well at least I'm home, sort of,
through them.
Am I angry? Yeah, course I am.
It was my life, and now it's gone. Pink mist.
I don't know—up here on Dundry Hill
things seem more clear,
and well, I guess I hope it'll change, somehow.
Till then, if people knew what it is,
that would be enough.
How the loss becomes the reason,
and how the reason's an abuse of love.
How here and there each wounding,
each death, resonates,
until millions are touched.
So that's all I hope for.
When the debate's being had,

the reasons given,
that people will remember
what those three letters mean,
before starting the chant once more—
Who wants to play war?
Who wants to play war?

The sound of wind on a high hill, fading

Acknowledgements

I am indebted to the many service personnel and their families whose stories have informed this work, especially Lyndon Chatting-Walters and Daniel Shaw, whose own experiences are, at times, closely echoed in these pages.

Pink Mist would not exist had it not been for the vision and support of Tim Dee of BBC Bristol, who first commissioned and guided the work towards broadcast.

Lastly, I would like to thank Lee Brackstone and Becky Fincham of Faber, Nan Talese, my agents Zoë Waldie and Zoë Pagnamenta, Clare Pollard, Chris Terrill, Ken Hames and, as ever, Katherine Eluned for her listening, advice and belief.

A Note About the Author

Owen Sheers is a poet, author, and playwright. His awards for poetry and drama include the Somerset Maugham Award for *Skirrid Hill*, the Hay Festival Medal for Poetry and Welsh Book of the Year for *Pink Mist*, and the Amnesty International Freedom of Expression Award for his play *The Two Worlds of Charlie F.* He is the author of two novels: *I Saw a Man*, shortlisted for the Prix Femina Étranger, and *Resistance*, which was translated into ten languages and adapted into a film. *The Dust Diaries*, his Zimbabwean nonfiction narrative, won the Welsh Book of the Year Award in 2005. He lives in Wales with his wife and daughter. He has been a New York Public Library Cullman Fellow and is currently Professor in Creativity at Swansea University.

A Note About the Type

The text of this book was set in Sabon, a typeface designed by Jan Tschichold (1902–1974), the well-known German typographer. Designed in 1966 in Frankfurt, Sabon was named for the famous Lyons punch cutter Jacques Sabon.